tongue & toe

Guess In The Row

Satyendra

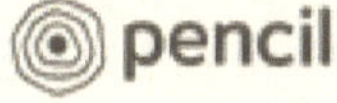

ISBN 978-93-5458-357-5

Published in India 2021 by Pencil

A brand of
One Point Six Technologies Pvt. Ltd.
123, Building J2, Shram Seva Premises,
Wadala Truck Terminal, Wadala (E)
Mumbai 400037, Maharashtra, INDIA
E connect@thepencilapp.com
W www.thepencilapp.com

Author biography

Satyendra Yadav Yes its me, is a writer of different kind, actually every writer has their own philosophy and so i am. I have catered you a number of short stories, like hard heart, Toilet and Ladies, Sadagi, Afwah etc. I use to maintain blogs sattupujari.blogspot.com. and satyendrastories.blogspot.com

I do not get the platform to publish my stories and my novel offline in the Indian market as it is very costly and tough to get it publish. Therefore I decided to publish it online and finally i thought of kindle, and now amazon started to publish a paperback also it also a tremendous step towards aspirant like me. initially i published my most of the work at kindle but now i step towards Pencil and other plateform.

Female Male or Both is a novel written by Satyendra thats me, this novel is actually about the philosophy involve in hermaphrodites hermaphrodites who they are complete human beings. like they dont need to complete themselves with their male or female parts further story unwrap and the novel story tells about the imagination and the possibility of life style if there is no disturbance of counter sex in human life. This novel involves in a world where living creatures don't have to maintain the sex ratio, even they are not afraid of being rape. Committing rape or maintaining sex ratio is like a joke among the society,

because the living creature exists in the form of hermaphrodite. You can get the flavour of different world and their priorities.
and the second one is Shokha: in the search of soul, which reveals that there is energy in the environment it depends on you how you are going to use it.
and now this is. if you want to read more about me visit facebook.com/b01satyendra.

CONTENTS

“You are in exact shape

I wanted my hands on your breast if it's the kind of love you wanted to do.
Maybe it's later or very soon but I wanted your love at night or noon.
I wanted to coincide our love without any scientific tool,
let me perform this love, it does not matter if it's May or June.
Do you mind if love begins at nine, and the love I wanted to do there is no end game sign?

"Love I wanted to do"

I wanted my hands on your breast if it's a kind of love you wanted to do.
Maybe it's later or very soon but I wanted your love at night or noon.
I wanted to coincide our love without any scientific tool,
let me perform this love, it does not matter if its May or June.
Do you mind if love begins at nine, and the love I wanted to do there is no end game sign.

"She is tasteless"

Pls, give me permission, to show my heart situation.
You are there as a wonderful fear,
The fear for me to lose you somewhere.
Coz it is you who lighten the sphere.
Before your admission my face was in gloom and heart was in tear.
It (my heart) like the way you travel in its terrain.
It needs your permission to wake up you again.

"Digital Love"

What would I say about justice in digitalization?
Does every act require social media attention to judge anything?
It cant be the real modernization.
Where is the law and where is order and what is doing the administration.
Now the society is in hands of those digitals crowed, which has no brain,
if it has then the "main Bhi chowkidar" campaign does not get fail due to automation...
Is it right the decision left on two digits(0,1)? Where is gravity, provoke, and grudges in which influence crime has been committed has no limits?

"She is a question mark"

Who are you?
My love or a stranger who knocked at its door.
You came into my life like a sparkle,
But your intention was really unknown which seems like a question mark?
Initially, we started following each other sitting alongside submitting the notes
But the way you approached me made me a joke.
I always consider you like those untouched petals of a lotus,
but your behavior proved that you are a disbalance rhombus.
Yes I like you, I want to talk to you more and more
I want to spend time with you more and more,
But it does not mean you make me feel like I am nothing to you and started me ignore.
If you have ever tried my heart taste it contains with the love of ocean which I wanted to pour.

"Limitless love"

If my love anyhow could be less for you, I can invest some more.
I love you the way the ocean loves the shore.
You were the world of my life which I wanted to design.
I created a world for you and you scattered my idea and say that I don't need it I am just fine.
Maybe my love does not suit you or it cants perfectly align.

"A barren love"

Does love matters to you or your heart become barren?
I tried to touch your heart but I failed to blow the love of siren.
It may be I am not your type, but tell me about yours, I swear you to become something more.
You are the only addiction like a pet in my life,
It will be a curse if I fail to make you my wife.
I always tried my best to complete the work maybe my life is in danger or my heart is on the knife.
I love you beyond my life….

Innocent love

How is it possible not to think of you?
My every deed has your essence, its every step is a touch of your love.
If I think of anything it seems like it never gets completed without you. And people say I am partial.
Maybe I am partial or inclined towards your thoughts,
but I can't do anything in it because it is you who can accelerate and moderate my thought.
I am no one without you.
You and I are like a companion, which cannot be separated at any cost.
It seems a little exaggerated, but anyhow if you can feel my heart then you will understand the deeper place for you.

"Hidden Love"

Should I think like you, to get the love you have stolen inside your heart?
How I can uncover those love for me?
Teach me the tricks which can strike on those blanket of thoughts to cut it in pieces to find those love.
My cells are dying without your love, oh my darling comes a bit closer and let the fountain of your love fall over.
These droplets of your love falling every pore of my thirsty organs.
And your love is falling so gradual and simultaneous on my feelings which finishes its thirst dipper in my heart.
But still, the fear of it is losing the essence of your love can be abolished because I doubt my response to your love.
Because in overjoy my heart forgets its limit and its behaviour comes in the category of malfunction.
Anyway, I will try not to behave illicitly, but this discipline crush my joy and without discipline, I can't get those what I want.

"Scientific Love"

Should I think like you, to get the love you have stolen inside your heart?
How I can uncover those love for me?
Teach me the tricks which can strike on those blanket of thoughts to cut it in pieces to find those love.
My cells are dying without your love, oh my darling comes a bit closer and let the fountain of your love fall over.
These droplets of your love falling every pore of my thirsty organs.
And your love is falling so gradual and simultaneous on my feelings which finishes its thirst dipper in my heart.
But still, the fear of it is losing the essence of your love can be abolished because I doubt my response to your love.
Because in overjoy my heart forgets its limit and its behavior comes in the category of malfunction.
Anyway, I will try not to behave illicitly, but this discipline crushes my joy and without discipline, I can't get those that I want.

"Rational Love"

Why am I weeping?
Is it those tears that are dropping coz someone scratches my heart at those places where it feels weakness
nd she got to know about the weak wall of my heart.
How she hammered on it? Did her hands not tremble?
Did she never think about that frequency which makes her remember me which generated from the beats of my heart?
This heart which beats on her memory on the occasion when it feels that she is about to knock on it.
This knocking starts when her lips move the movement of her lips makes it dance but does it matter for her who crushed it beneath her feet.

"Men are victim of marriage"

After the marriage, you left your home.
And what about me? Me too left my home coz you can't let your feet inside my home.
My home echoed you, you don't like the way you got treatment here coz this is not your own home.
And in this home need an special treatment for you.
My father is Ravan brother is Kumhkarn and my sister pretending Supernakha for you.
Think about my situation what shaped a creation in you?
Only they are good who related to you before marriage,
I am nothing to you and my relatives are garbage to you.

Don't blame me

After the marriage, you left your home.
And what about me? Me too left my home coz you can't let your feet inside my home.
My home echoed you, you don't like the way you got treatment here coz this is not your own home.
And in this home need a special treatment for you.
My father is Ravan brother is Kumhkarn and my sister pretending Supernakha for you.
Think about my situation what shaped a creation in you?
Only they are good who related to you before marriage,
I am nothing to you and my relatives are garbage to you.

"Ocean of love"

All the love in you like you are the origin of love.
You love the people who have nothing in return.
How the people can claim you are greedy and keep antidote with you?
You are the cleanser, who cleans my soul.
It seems to love to me but thought it could be infatuation like your name.
I started poetry a new and passionate game.
If it's a game, what would be the result if I would do the same?
I never care for the result but always loved your name.

"My wild desire"

I will be there to fuck you, my dear
Why to fuck coz it is you who compelled me to do.
Otherwise, I don't have the desire, to set you on fire.
Your hands-on my jeans moving to smear.
You are so lair hiding desire, talk to your heart open your shirt. Let me begin by pulling you near.
It needs your submission, let me handle the situation.
You are going out of control let me decide the gear and engage you from the rear.
Maybe it's tough for you but it is those which make your mind clear.
Forget the fear let me fire the rear,
Hold your tear coz it led you to the extreme orgasm which you always whisper in my ear....in my ear....

"Me & worth"

I have to make it straight the thing lying between my legs, otherwise, you will get calm and leave me for someone else.

"Pain in my heart"

I know You bleed every month, and what about mine ejaculate to make you feel orgasm?
You always need a muscular man to feel you the Param Sukh,
you never cared about my feelings if I am lean n thin.
To make you feel orgasm I tried a lot, roam around the medicine shop and Vadya Rahmani hut.

"she is everything to me"

You were my gain, you are my loss.
I am so twig, you are so large.
I could not understand your situation when I was following my heart.
You are the angel you can forgive if the boundary has been crossed.
I have listened to the girl they clean so fast,
pls don't clean your heart maybe I m there like dust.
Put me in the bin of your heart
but don't through me outside.
Even the bin can feel your breadth,
It is not necessary to go in straight, run continuously,
And never look back if the journey is long why to make it hard?
We are the organizer we can again start.

"Supreme Love"

Love yourself you are the supreme.
Uncover the space like you have done it in a dream.
How anyone can claim your superiority?
They have to follow your intellectual stream.
Everyone is beneath you and you can do whatever you want if it needs to go in the extreme.
Love needs no permission to travel up or downstream.
Love is the ultimate goal of life how anyone could claim its ownership?
You are very much fertile to grow the love and if the land is yours you have the ownership.
You can love the nature too because you are from nature and nature from you.
And this love would be maintained from generation to generation.
And if anyhow your love gets diverted to lust, Its all happen when you don't need salvation.

"Fire in the heart"

You are like a professional and greedy doctor who spread the virus and the antidote is only with them,
it's just like that my heart is pinching inside it.
Is it you or something else?
There is no cure for it, it was nice that I could have taken precautions coz it is better than a cure.
And the antidote is with you, for God shake forget your greed and make available the cure.
Otherwise, I will be no more.

"Care for Love"

Love and fear mostly I got in you, it seems like life is name before your name and only fear of not to disappear.
It's not like these love and fear which made you clear but all those things are not so visible and as your image are made up of love.
Why you are so faithful and the world seems mountains of betrayal?
It may because I don't deserve their love and you don't deserve my betrayal.
Betrayal comes from the heart, how does it come from the heart if it is made to respond to the blood,
Its because blood flow as per the thoughts, and my thoughts begins and ends at you.
And if this is the way I can have your name in my blood vessel, I will chant your name every time, it may be day or night.

"Reason & love"

Love and fear mostly I got in you, it seems like life is the name before your name and only fear of not to disappear.
It's not like these love and fear which made you clear but all those things are not so visible and as your image are made up of love.
Why you are so faithful and the world seems mountains of betrayal?
It may because I don't deserve their love and you don't deserve my betrayal.
Betrayal comes from the heart, how does it come from the heart if it is made to respond to the blood,
It's because blood flow as per the thoughts, and my thoughts begin and end at you.
And if this is the way I can have your name in my blood vessel, I will chant your name every time, it may be day or night.

"From the corner of my heart"

How I can forget those bright nights when we taste each other.
And it's today there is a fear I may not have get disappear.
It seems like a glacier has been collapsed with my heart
Which became cold and be again start.
It seems like there is a fearful pain in my breath,
When its molecule comes in contact it eroded the space
And feels like a crane is pulling my heart, which really hurts.

"It's my heart not your husband"

"It's my heart not your husband"
It's not about you, it's my heart sometimes its don't listen to me then who the hell are you?
It's my heart it's, not your husband and most important that it's not the henpecked one.
It is my eyes it's not your servant.
It may be my mind bounds to you, it may be my lips give smile to you.
But it's my hands which shows my strength
It does not follow ur charm, it has a job to follow my heart.
Which is not ur husband…
It is my heart it's not your bride.
It is still a virgin which makes me feel pride.
It is my heart which needs a new start.
It's my legs it's not your car.
It's my ear it's not your student to hear.
It's my tongue it's not your lab to taste the junk.
It's my nose it smells so well but I am so sorry it's can't taste you coz you are not the rose…you are not the rose….
It's my heart it's not your husband…

"Suitable Love"

O God give me the love which suits me.
I would never ask for her figure, it's her heart which I want to see.

"Crush in the class"

You are the girl from whom I want to be inspired.
I want to see a single hand raised in the class to snatch the attention to show her desire.
It's a desire to learn and teach not to tag, share and subscribe which make me tired.
You are special who think before the act, which is followed by legends, not by a lair.
Leave the world, every particle has conspired.
It is you to whom I wanted to admire.
It is you to whom I wanted to admire...
What is life? If you think you are enjoying.
What is the joy of life if you did not touch the spiritual fire?
Find the peace search the real happiness which can't be flown by your physical desire.....

"Crush in class II"

Your name stands infatuation to me.
Your eyes are the most beautiful creation to me.
Your smile creates a confusing situation for me.
Do a favour give me your fever, I want to snatch your grief and pull you near.
Hold your face forget the fear.
Close your eyes let the innocence disappear.
To make you naughty remove your tear.
You asked me to describe you in my poetry.
I searched my knowledge and reminded the Shakespeare.
I call you again my angel and you told me your dear.
I jumped over the chair when the words come to my ear.
You are really my angel but I can't be your dear.

"Crush in College"

Your name stands infatuation to me.
Your eyes are the most beautiful creation to me.
Your smile creates a confusing situation for me.
Do a favour give me your fever, I want to snatch your grief and pull you near.
Hold your face forget the fear.
Close your eyes let the innocence disappear.
To make you naughty remove your tear.
You asked me to describe you in my poetry.
I searched for my knowledge and reminded Shakespeare.
I call you again my angel and you told me your dear.
I jumped over the chair when the words come to my ear.
You are really my angel but I can't be your dear.

"tongue & toe"

If you will allow my tongue, it wants to go deeper in you.
It will taste u in every nooks and corner of you.
It travels from the brow, and reach to the toe.
In the journey of its, it will go high and ditch by moving too slow.
Some of them to chew, some are to bite rest are to swallow in the full moon night.
It's the tongue who needs your permission, assume the rest who will come in addition.

"Romance in arms"

Come in my arms, and let me feel you.
I want to reach to your soul.
That is neither my destiny nor my goal.
It is the first milestone in my journey to you.
If you will allow I will touch your soul.

"After the first chat with her"

Pls, give me permission, to show my heart situation.
You are there as a wonderful fear,
The fear for me to lose you somewhere.
Coz it is the you who lighten the sphere.
Before your admission my face was in gloom and heart was in tear.
It (my heart) like the way you travel in its terrain.
It needs your permission to wake up you again.

"My first love"

You are the angel of my life, who torch the way I was going in the night.

You bring a smile again on my face, you changed the competition in the race.

I started following your action, I learnt to struggle with the situation.

These four days were not common for me, I m yours and you are sawan to me.

You jerk my heart from inner, before your glance I was a sinner.

This sin will be finished and illuminate like a pearl, give me your heart and I will be your sinner.

"you are made up of love"

You are the shape of love, if love persists anywhere it is within you.
This shape is not about the curves you got.
This is all about the depth of your heart and height of your thought.
I always remind your appearance in my dream. Which may be your thought which can't be seen.

"Random thoughts"

Your bare legs reminded me of autumn.
Autumn may be dull and full of gloom.
But your beauty doesn't even care for the season; it always creates a reason to follow you.
The power of your beauty is always constant; it never gets alter either in summer or in winter.
I am so jealous of summer which doesn't allow me to love as in winter.

"BETTER LOVE"

I don't want to love you, even its not my hobby.
I am so stupid, I can't follow my brain it's my heart who want you again.
I persuade it even bribe it not to follow the same.
Because neither you are so beautiful nor so young.
I surprise with its reply, which claims your pure thoughts and melodious voice.
It's my heart which is not in my control who wanted to soluble in your thought and touch your soul.

MASTURBATION

Pls, give me permission, to show my heart situation.
You are there as a wonderful fear,
The fear for me to lose you somewhere.
Coz it is the you who lighten the sphere.
Before your admission, my face was in gloom and my heart was in tear.
It (my heart) like the way you travel in its terrain.
It needs your permission to wake up you again.

"HER HAPPINESS"

I always thought that how I would make her happy?
Where is the happiness, what is secret of her happiness? I will make her happy forever.
Foods that don't make her happy.
Caring yes I thought it would make her happy, but what kind of caring? How should I care for her these all are an illusion? My favorite's jokes cant made to show her teeth, but it is real that a happy woman is a myth.

"BED & YOU"

Do you really like my dickk?
Or it's me who is in inferior complex and thinking you needs a large and thick.
Why do you cry when the moan can cover scene,
You should not cry coz it is so twig it is so thin.
You think I am stupid making me a fool,
Maybe you have a better idea of orgasm coz I have not attended the sexual school.
You can be the master in bed and perform so well.
I am not very hot I am so cool.

"In the society of feminist"

Most of the women can't be sexually satisfied by their men and what they told that they are the sexual victim.
Who is guilty if she did not get the orgasm?
Is it my penis or the spasm due to sexual activism?
She has a problem with all those things which a woman needs in her eroticism.
And she makes me feel like I am doing something like terrorism.
Who is guilty if a penis is a weapon my gaze are like bullets and hands are sword it seems like I am mobile war tourism.
If you think it is a crime to posses my own organs with me the kind sexual conflict can't be resolved on the platform of feminism.

A LETTER TO CONFUSED (me)

Does that love mean to you? anything? Why this "self" is so involved in you and if this "self" is so involved it must be spiritual.

Otherwise what is the use of its if it is following the physical and virtual dimension of life.

It may happen that these following physical things please you instantly. But it can not give you for what you are here, it's neither actual nor real.

It's tough to decide for what we are here?

But it's sure that neither a penis nor a penny can justify our existence in this atmosphere.

It's not the globe which can decide our existence, coz who the hell know how many globes have been disappeared in this sphere.

A MOM OF A MARRIED BOY

Mom I love you, may I really love you the way you wanted me to love?
I am not able to understand your need of love.
Maybe I am not your favorite child,
Maybe these all are an illusion of my mind.
But for what you biased me and did not save the equal part of love.
I am sure that it's not your mistake, maybe my brother and sister need it more.
Its not my mistake if I am married.
She too is the mother of my child but I did not see favourable or partial love in her heart.
Maybe she has a single child or she is not the mother in-law.

"a fedup married boy"

These relations like mother, father and sisters are complications.

To solve it I have attended many seminars and workshop sessions.

But I did not got success because wife and mother have a difference in generation.

Wife is wife and mother is mother but I am the husband and son who has to handle the situation.

She thinks it's her charm which snatched my attention.

And she that her chanted hymn which made me blind.

But I want to ask who am I, who will decide?

Who has given me right to make her slave.

Its her life let her live anywhere.

You are the mother of mine, she is no one who can give you a favour. You may be innocent, but she too has not the crocodile tear.

The story does not end here or there.

She does some other things and you mix some spices and spread it everywhere.

"I was too young to make you addiction"

These suffering these loneliness and you.
These all are painful but you are the most.
I am searching the soul who makes me the whole.
You gave me the joy between your thighs; I reached in the ditch though I wanted to fly high.
The height you shown me that to my tongue for that I was too young.
Soon you became the guardian of my thought.
You make me feel the fantasies in fool moon night.
In those nights you and I get much closer with open eyes.
I starred on your body and taste with my gaze it was so crispy and full of spices.
This taste was not so common which can be finished in a single gulp, but I had to indulge my whole young energy to fill my stomach.

"Spiritual Goal"

Is it necessary to roam inside your heart, or your body is enough to suck the nectar of love.
If your heart leads to the spirituality what kind of love reach to that status?
That Sufi love needs no entrance to get inside you and reach to the soul.
Life contains those loves in it but it does not get displays due to distances more and more.
Do you really believe in those which begin from eyes and ends to the soul?
I really does not get its concept where neither a fantasies nor any romantic goal.
Somewhere I listened in this love your thoughts plays a great role.
I am blind in this path torch to the eternal goal.

"First Love Fight"

You are so ugly you are so cheap.
I am so smooth I am so clean.
Don't so my limit, I touched infinite.
You are in the dark corner where neither a glimpse nor a sight.
Why do you make a fuss of mine to create a drama and leave my sign.
I will never forgive you for this crime, if I would be a judge you would be hung.

"Desired Girl"

Yes, she has beautiful eyes and hair.
I love her so much she doesn't even care.
Her eyes are black and hair are curly.
To find a glimpse of her I wake so early.
She is so cute she is so dear, she lives in my heart which is very close and near.
I am the fool who searches her everywhere.
Her cheeks are pink and lips are purple.
I roam for a glimpse of her here and there making a circle.
How would I say she is my angel, though she is me I am no one without her love affair.

"tinder sex and love"

What can we expect from a girl on tinder?
Who knows what she is searching for a mighty heart or a broken penis?
Yes, it's not her mistake if she is on tinder, she may be there to hold a macho hand there's nothing to wonder.
But what the mistake of mine if I consider her a pond of love and the love of mine has been surrender.
Maybe I have a broken penis but it does not mean I have done a blunder.
She can have a shallow vagina or the vagina who don't have a place to create a space, I am so sick of her who wants to earn her like Sikandar.
She can't be innocent only coz she is in the possession of a pair of breast and a hole for sex.
Yes, it's not the sex which pleases me in bed let me rest.
I am the man who can enjoy myself after masturbate.

"An application to Love"

You are so ugly you are so cheap.
I am so smooth I am so clean.
Don't so my limit, I touched infinite.
You are in the dark corner where neither a glimpse nor a sight.
Why do you make a fuss of mine to create a drama and leave my sign?
I will never forgive you for this crime, if I would be a judge you would be hung.

Her expectation

There is every big myth about the marriage that you will be happy.
Why happy marriage is a myth because the expectations you have for her or his
Expectations ruin marriages.
Expectations ruin life
Expectation make happy marriage is myth.
Lets talk about some silly things
She expects me to live with her without my parents.
Destroy all the connections and live with her.
Never talk to your parents your talk to her's.
Never gift your sisters just please her's.
She expects me fight with your parents on her command.
She expect me to do all the domestic work without her request.
She expects me keep quite if she insulted me in-front of people.
Why do you expect me if you do the same and begin the blame game.
You may be somewhere right but your approach push me towards the shame.
How could you be so happy to hurt me?

Orgasm

Hello why cant you hold my hand, you are the best thing happens to me.
Lets move on road my hand in your hand and synching the steps.
A single icecream squze we both.
Then my hand in your waist and move a little away.
The palm slipped a bit and touched your thigh.
This is not only way to make you shy
My elbow touched your butt, which gave you the sign.
Move a little there is some darkness which our private friend.
Lets go with this friend and witness it the love we have.
don't you dare to moan darkness may not listen but the walls have ear.
I don't want to ruin your reputation because I do have care.
Unwrap your saree and let me wrap you in my arms.
Let me taste you till your orgasm I know the place where to place my palm.
don't close your eyes darkness is our friend it will help you to be calm.
My fingers my lips my tongue and teeth are in the service of your orgasm.

come closer to me

Come closer to me show your emotion to me.
Lets fill the gap start a rap lets be cozy with me.
Your arms your legs your hips and breasts.
Lets feel it all and try the next.
Get closer to me little bit closer to me.
Lets smear my hands in your skin tight pants.
Lets move it and tear your braw straps.
Lets do it and do it.
Its time to do it.
Show me the rest
I will do my best
Just show me yes just show me.
I am here to help
don't be panic I am not going to test.
Just do it lets do it.

forget the p

She is incomplete without he
And he is incomplete without she.
We both are searching our destiny.
We have lost our half
She may be confuse he may be rude.
She can say I am your better half you are my dude.
She is mislead on the road of dark.
He is somewhere trying to convince and talk.
We both are suffering due to this lost.
Let's have a hug together forget the past.

Rapist got blind

Yes I am young and sexy, my breast appears on my tops
my hips are visible on my jeans but my lips are not
open to suck.
Maybe my looks are sluty in your definition but it does not mean my jeans are open for your cock.
It's me who can act as per my mind my thought is not so weak which can be lock.
My freedom cant be tolerated by you, how it can offend your dick to rape and fuck?
No, it's not the fault of your dick, it's your eyes that give tears in mine.
So if your eyes are guilty the punishemt must be given to thine.
Your eyes must not remain in this world which would create a holy sign.
This would be justice if your sight would be snatched and you will be blind, you will blind.

Girls are rare

Most of the girls locked their profiles on Facebook.
Instagram is just a tool to increase their followers.
Tinder needs something which can't be spare.
I tried on most of the girls but I did not get my match.
Then finally I met a woman but she had responsibilities to catch.
She is a perfect match but her responsibilities through my mind away.
She is stuck in the match and her life and she has no words to say.
This is a situation that can't be admired.
Once I thought of her that she will never let me in her heart.
I don't know if there is a space for me the way I thought in her heart.
She is like dream to me which can't be shared.
I like the way she moves and walks, I like the way she thinks and talks.
She may be the perfect match but she is locked.
She has responsibilities that make me mad so I think my mind needs a repaird.

"Transexual Love"

Who am I?
you are a trans yes you are a trans.
You can't fuck even you can't hold mine which a girl can accommodate without any fear or terrific sign,
You are good for nothing why are you here you are a trans u should not cross the line.
You are incomplete by nature how can u stand with us within the line,
I did not understand the purpose y you are here?
Neither I m incomplete nor a whore which should have a hole for ur pole,
Neither I need a dick nor a hole for my pole.
And I am here to engage the spiritual gear, neither to search a pole nor a hole.

Desire

You have a beautiful cleavage and the butt I like.
You came in my dream to demonstrate your ass.
Your ass came closer to me and hands got it job to make you moan.
Before your scream I wanted to finish.
Your pussy get weted my dick got lubricated.
You jumped over me and desire got deleted.

My dick

I have a desire which mostly get straight.
But my moral responsibility compelled me to make it down.
It get straight in the market, mall, class and mostly in the bed.
I tried alotz but it does not listen me.
This morality takes all the joy of its life.
He is dead now ,,, less hope to rezunuvate..
Pray for it..

www.ingramcontent.com/pod-product-compliance
Lightning Source LLC
LaVergne TN
LVHW050422160726
843469LV00041B/1194

* 9 7 8 9 3 5 4 5 8 3 5 7 5 *